MERRICK REESA ENERGY SOLUTION

The Solution To Government and Business Resources

BY:

Daniel W. Merrick, Ph.D.

© 2012 Daniel W. Merrick, PhD;
Eternal Light & Power Company Publishing
PO BOX 1533 Smethport, Pennsylvania 16749-1533

EternalLightAndPowerCompany.Org

Table of Contents

Preface..3
1 The Problem..4
The Problem in America....................................11
The Money Game...22
Energy and Resources......................................25
2 REESA Solution...27
PRA - Personal REESA Accounts....................28
BRA - Business REESA Accounts....................33
RRA - Real Estate REESA................................34
GRA - Government REESA..............................35
ETA - Emerging Technology REESA................35
REESA Legislation...37
CRA - Charity RESSA......................................38
SUMMARY OF POLICY...................................41
Conclusion..47
National Lottery..50
Last Page 56

Preface:

Read all this book!
Do not let your own opinions or perspective cloud your interpretation into something the author did not intend it to mean. Keep an open mind, and imagine that there is no doctrine to protect or dogma to uphold other than a solution must be obtained and implemented to insure mankind's survival.

If you can do this then you can become part of the solution instead of part of the problem.

The only way to surely fail is to never really try...

1 The Problem

We all know the problems that are becoming the issues of today's leading news stories, another failure of government economic systems that devalued assets. Greece, Spain, and the list goes on of countries that have had currency failures and riots in the streets as the people rise up in anger over failed leadership which lead to this crash.

In the United States the systems of government and politics has lead to a polarized extreme on each side with both failing to see the others perspectives and come to any agreements. But the root of these problems is not the solution to the problem nor is it the answer that will work in application to solving the problem.

In the world today we have two forms of government solutions which are both old ideas that I will prove by this book can not solve the problems of growing societies.

Those two sides we have called left and right, liberal and conservative, Communist and Capitalist. Doctrines of political science will say that there are differing forms, such as rule by democracy or allegory, republic and socialist, but in the end they all boil down to just two perspectives and points of view.

Communists have compiled into one group who

want to impose the group rule over others by the common pooling of resources for redistribution and management at government levels.

Capitalists want to allow individuals to own the resources and limit government from owning the means of production.

History has proven that when governments solve problems that they create two more problems that need solving and give the voters a new reason to vote them out of office.
I make no bones about my own position as a conservative. But you should not let that keep you from reading and applying these solutions to the problems. For some, a short history lesson in a more educated perspective may need to be addressed. let me enlighten you as to why this is needed today in this key time in man's history.

When I was born there was an Iron Curtain across Europe. In the west we had no mine fields, no machine gun pill boxes, and no razor sharp barbed wire keeping people from getting to the communist world. Yet the Communist world had these boarders which kept the people in.

We would see the news reports that showed those who risked their lives to get to freedom in hopes of being able to come to a better future. Many lost their lives trying to cross the boarder to freedom.

Since that time and after its popular knowledge of these events, many have been born. Liberal professors who think that the answer to the problems of government is the old solutions, which have failed in application, have been preaching from their pulpits at the universities that the communist ideal is a good one, but it has not been properly applied.

So many young people in this generation have not seen what the ends of the means of Communist ideals has always and always will result in. They have no point of reference in history to guide them and have no clue that the past left party was not so extreme and was just as capitalist as the right at one time.

All they see is what is put before their eyes so they see no need to avoid the Chi T-shirts because they did not see his murders or the dictators who ordered his death. As with Trotsky the young and uninformed do not know that the ultimate end of a communist and leftists government is always a dictatorship that will silence the most vocal of its voices when resources prevent the real implementation of the perfect ideals of societies relationships.
Capitalists also have their flaws in the actual practice of government which really equates to the same root problem with the left.

In Capitalism as it has been practiced you have an

opportunity for all to achieve any level of success. Yet the greed and exclusive nature of the ideas is limited by regulations, ownership of the ideas, and selective placement of resources to allow the most gifted ideas to come to the market.

The root of this problem where ever larger corporations share wealth through dividends was thought to be the solution to the clambering needs of the people to have a part in the free market society. So in the 1900s we saw the growth of industry and the corporate sharing of profits through the corporations laws that was a government regulation and law passed to impose a method to gain wide acceptance into a type of infrastructure within capitalism which mirrored in part the communist ideal of sharing the wealth. The idea was to limit the ability of one man or one company from gaining an exclusive market share and prevent an economic dictatorship.

Antitrust laws were also meant to solve the problem of one person or company having to much power over the people and controlling the economy. It was a way of putting your eggs in many baskets so when one failed there would still be others to take up the gap.

Some of these regulations seemed fair and gained wide acceptance by both sides of the issue, but still did not answer the root problem.

That root is greed and power. History has shown that the quote about absolute power corrupting absolutely is true in both methods of the solutions of the past.

In practice the left governments did not have enough resources so the middle management became discouraged and then corruption became common place. Extra payment for simple tasks of government in my wife's home country of Ukraine was filled with extra fees off the books during the Communist reign there. People did these things to survive and also to gain power over others. In a communist society where achievement is supposed to be equal, the only way to feel importance and belonging is to give others a reason to feel special about being your friend by the ability to do special favors, of course, for a extra fee.

By the same token the dictatorship or power exclusive factor in any form of government always rewards those who support their perspective. We see that in the United States where special interests and unions lobby officials for funding of their pet project to gain market share, political clout, and position.

In short, the problem with society is not government as a solution, but the heart of man and the greed and self actualization of corruption.

The Democrats in America say we need to get a

more equal playing field while the Republicans say we need to get a more equal opportunity with the distribution of wealth.

The real issue is not either point of view, but a more rational perspective to the problems with how mankind has solved this problem in the past and failed. History repeats itself has become a self fulfilling prophesy because that is how it has always been done.

I went some years back to my local representative in state government and presented my solution to him and this is what he said: "We will have to go to others states and see how they did this and find a way to make it work". Then over the next 4 years of his office he did nothing. The problem with the premise of finding a solution from what others are doing or have been doing in the past is that if that solution had worked, we would not be talking about how to solve the problem. It is just common senses of truth that when the solution is found that you need not look for the answer any more.

As any good political science major, my representative was using the applied instructions of failure to gain the answer that will insure you have a reason or problem that needs solved so that he can get elected again next voting season. Elections demand that he do this, and the structure of the system taught him to think that way.
Influence becomes the battle of popularity and that

is always resolved in the next election where we elect another incompetent political science major or lawyer to mix up the meaning of terms and words so as to say with assurance that his interpretation of the lie is so much better than his opponent.

The lie is that all men are by their nature dishonest. Unless a person has had a deep psychic experience as Freud put it, he is not changed in his heart and motivation. Self interest will always make the power elite to manipulate people to gain advantage in ownership of resources and wealth.

This comes from the sinful nature of mankind and the independent desire to rebel against God or the concept of God. People want to do what ever they want and not have anyone tell them they can not think the way or do what ever they want.
It is not a religious thing, it is a human nature thing. The concept of God is not what may be what a person is thinking of, but inside his conscience is treating him like a young child who is rebelling and that is what drives all humans in simple terms.

So if left or right by definition, we all have the same problem, we want more and to own more than others so we can feel special and some think that sharing will solve this problem and others think that giving others the means to solve the problem is enough.
In the practical application we have today a system

of governments world wide where by committees they control the absolute power from gaining control and doing what men like Hitler did in outlawing a race of people. Stalin did the same thing on a greater scale than Hitler when he starved to death millions of Ukrainians during his rule. Each year in Ukraine they celebrate the starvation Holocaust where millions of family members died because of the food shortage where Russia took away all the crops and left nothing for the Ukrainian people.

"Absolute power corrupts absolutely"

There have been other holocausts also where for political dogmas men have exterminated other men for what they think. We need not address these in a list here if one has just read some good history books that do not slant ideas toward a left or extreme ignorance of the truth. This is why there is a 2nd Amendment.

The Problem in America

We can use the recent news and healthcare issue to gain insight into what the polarization has created in the United States and find our solution from a real rational answer.

The democrats wanted a health care bill that would give everyone medical services and allow persons to get abortions or birth control, as they call it dishonestly, according to their personal choice.

The republicans wanted to limit the health care to spiritual choice of the individual to prevent personal resource from going to abortions so as to protect the constitution rights of personal freedoms of religion. That is why we have a 1st Amendment.

A free market solution insuring the capitalists view was mixed into the pot of communist ideas and out came the Obamacare bill that was forced down the republicans throat.

The Catholic Church filed suit along with others to change the law into a personal religious freedom choice to support the ideal of the Godless left that forced the spiritual to give up their belief for the government imposed act of killing by abortion. The disagreement prevails and depending on who wins the election we are supposed to think that this problem will be solved by our side getting control of the system for 4 more years.

The reality is that if you left the unborn to grow and allowed nature to take it's course, there would be a human life in 9 months. The only real reason to prevent that from happening is if a person or nature does something to stop that from happening.

No matter what each side thinks, the real truth is that the only reason for government to be in this equation is if the child born will be a cost to the government. Further more if you look at the only real reason to not have a child it would be that the child will not have enough to eat and survive.

In Darwinist terms the survival of the child depends on resources.

In Israel there is a group who in place of having the disagreement to the abortion problem and funding they have formed a charity that gives the resource to the mother so she can keep her baby and not have to worry if there will be enough food and clothing. They solved the problem of what the real issue of abortion is by removing the problem of the mother's mind by pooling resources into a package source of food and clothing to meet the needs of the mother and child before she is forced by her perception of circumstances to get an abortion.

This seems to me to be the more truthful approach and remove the argument of who's right to choose it is.

Still in the United State we have the problem that spiritual people do not want to pay taxes to governments who will use the money for abortion or birth control which opposes their personal spiritual beliefs.

By the constitution they should have that right to

make that choice. The left says no you have to do it my way or else. The right says no way and when they shift power will undo that which the left has done. Back and forth this goes each 4 years and nothing is accomplished in solving the rights of individuals in choosing there own personal free way of worship, or not worshiping at all at the alter of the constitution religion.

Those who think bigger government is the solution to the problem lack faith in the people that we can direct the paths of our own lives and choices and those who think less government lack trust that the big government folks will understand that the nanny state will consider the long term issues that cause government to fail in respecting the individual and the rights the constitution gives.

These rights do not come from government, they come from God or nature which displays that we have the right to act and do what ever we choose within the law. Changing the laws to allow for chaos to force change will only destroy society and lead back to the dark ages of kings and dictators where the state was run by religions and by sovereign rule.

This problem is the endless circle of never addressing the individual rights and allowing powerful influence to dictate policy by the means to control the lobbyists and the message in media and in the press. This is why our founders instilled the freedom of speech and the press to allow the people to choose by popular opinion those issues that would make laws within the bodies of congress and the senate to insure one person's rights would not usurp another person's rights and freedom. As in life, liberty, and the pursuit of happiness the law against murder prevents others from taking life from someone with the threat of equal justice by execution.

I personally do not want to pay for someone to execute their unborn child with my tax dollars. I personally do not want to be judged on judgment day before God for having been a part of that person's personal choice to not have that child. I also do not want to see a mother have to give up that child's life because she is not wealthy enough to feed the child in the monitory system that mankind has agreed to play the money game under. I would rather than see this issue even have to be addressed, that she make the personal choice to use birth control before the baby is conceived or have enough to feed and care for the child when it is born.

Under my plan that would become the personal responsibility of the individual and my tax dollars would never have to come to the table in any event that I disagreed with on a spiritual bases having the rights of the constitution protecting my right to worship with my dollars where I feel they should show support.

Like wise under my plan those who choose otherwise would become personally responsible for their own choices in this matter and I would no longer be part of the equation. Likewise the government should not be involved in it also. Government by the constitution should not be providing health care, retirement funding, or any personal choice under my plan, just regulating the laws and boundaries by which we govern our money system to allow for fairness for both capitalism and communism in it's best forms to thrive in society without having to readdress the same issues over and over about who's ideas work best to govern the people by the people.

We the people should be governed by the people, for the people, without intrusive rules and regulations that are to costly to administer and to cumbersome to implement.

The ideals of the communist principles of sharing is lofty in perfect practice and among many religious groups that Marx observed in forming his ideas would be great in practice if everyone loved everyone else and all got along. But we live in the real world where the ideas of the Bible where it says "they held all things in common" would be great if all could be cooperative in all things, but in practice, personal property is just a fact of biology.

Sanitation it self requires that we do not share our toothbrush to avoid the spreading of disease. It becomes obvious the problems of sharing when we see the lack of application by the richest advocates to this type of society in practice of their ideals. George Soros claims to want the left form of a socialist state but still maintains his billionaire empire of wealth pretending that his goals would be to liquidate his wealth and share it with everyone.

Yet he has not done that, nor will he, because he is just a manipulator rather than a truly faithful to the cause of the communist ideals. He in fact does not want a equal sharing system but a dictatorship where he owns everything and everyone and is the dictator. If he really believed in communism and the left's principals then he would become equally poor with the rest of us and share equally all his wealth.

The same is true of many billionaires like Oprah and even millionaires like Bill Maher and many Hollywood leftists. Even the professors at the universities that seek to brainwash the young to a leftist point of view do not really practice their religion of sharing in truth. The real enemies of human nature which causes this is that envy, status, position, power, and the bully pulpit commands a personal actualization that gives them a freedom of influence above that of the common man and woman. This is what drives and motivates them into the lime light of popular opinion and the stage. The root of that effect is the psychology of

Ego and always with ego you can only have one god, even if it is a tin god of their own empires in segments of society.

Interesting enough with the self serving empires of the capitalist world we find the same self-importance with the economic empires where ever more and greater wealth and achievement is a badge of importance and recognition that drives from the same human nature.

The self and it's greed to gain position and importance is replaced for the solution which I have in this book in both cases which leads to one answer at the root of the last 100 years of dishonest reporting of the facts to spin and twist things to ones own perspective of the issues.

That root issue is a simple question which the founders solved and did work well for most of the life of this nation. That is they stated in the documents of founding that we are one nation under God. The left has been trying to redefine God and who he is and if he exists. The motive is that they want to be God and can not be God if there is one true God.

The point is not that you believe in God or not, but that we should all agree that we are not God. If we think there is no God then we are not him if He is. Nor should we force others to believe there is not a God by changing the rules of the founders to come up with the state as God or any leader as God. Thus Government is not God, nor is science, nor is anything God but God if He is and if we can agree that we are not God then we have begun to find the solution rather than the problem.

If I want to teach my children there is a God, you have no right to tell me not to do that, limit my free speech to do that in schools, or dictate by any law that doing such is a violation of your rights. Nor do I have the right to force you and your children to be subject to my free speech that you have to do the opposite. In fact, lets now agree that you can teach there is no God and I can teach there is, and we should let our children be subject to our personal preferences until they are of age and can decide for themselves.

The only reason for wanting to force your views on my children would be to use them to reach some desired end of your own opinion or use. To do that would be selfish and manipulative and would not be truly allowing for freedom of speech. Regardless of the system of worship or non worship, we should all just agree that the founders were in fact Christians and Jews who founded us as one nation under God and we are not Him. The State is not God and can not solve every problem, nor is any system of government a solution to the problem because the government has shown that it is the problem.

Religion is not the problem, and faith or beliefs outside of religions is not the problem, but the freedom to find your own truth is the solution in the present world and that is why I am writing this book.

I am the father of a child with a disability who has Duchennes' Muscular Dystrophy. I do not expect that the problem of his slow dying should be the financial responsibility of the state, or you in any way. I do hope that you will be compassionate and allow him to live and survive until a cure is created or until God heals him. If you do not believe in God then I hope you would just care because he is a member of mankind and he is a small part of society at large and would understand the joy that his life has given to me and our family. I do not think it is government who will solve his problem and in most cases I think government would not solve his problems. But I don't want to see the solution that Hitler had for such as my son, nor do I want to impose on your family to meet my families needs. I just want the right to resources that will allow me to have the same capitalistic means of production that George Soros has so I can provide from my child and family.

I want to inspire a debate that will solve my problem along with setting the tone for an open minded discussion about the solution. So if you are from the left, and do not believe the bible as I do, then at least we can agree that the stories in the bible have a morality that we all can learn, and like a Hollywood movie, perhaps we can bring out the better nature of us all to allow for the right thing to be done in the end. For example the story of Cain and Able in Genesis. Cain made an offering that was not acceptable and Able made an offering that was accepted. Cain became jealous of Able and killed him. It is a type of metaphor about human nature and even our personal struggles in life to gain wealth, position and fame. Everyone wants to be liked and accepted and when we are not we get angry and fight for some sort of place in life to find friendship and acceptance.

This same theme of our story is played out every four years in the election process where Cain kills Able and we try to find a better leadership that will accept our offering and we all will gain a reward of recognition in doing the right thing as we see it.

But the real roots of what is happening is we do not find acceptance by all, and we continue the fight where one side gets there way and the others get killed every four years. The real way to solve the problem is to find out what works and keep it without having to change roles every time to see whose offering will be accepted each term.

I may hate your offering and think I can fight God over the issue, but I don't really have to kill you to get a compromise with life on life's terms. In government this is true also.

Only in cooperation and in the joy of the solution in cooperative work can any society find happiness. When our favorite team wins we all find joy and celebration in the cooperation that coordinates the way we play the game and share in the rewards of victory.

So lets give up our old way of doing things and find the solution so we can enjoy the rewards of victory without killing Able again every time an offering is required.

As a Messianic Jew I have my beliefs and faith, and arguments with differing religious doctrines. I do not have to go over to the Catholic church and force everyone there to accept my faith under the threat of death. In politics it is the same principals of the game that can be applied in government that can find a team work effort that can bring the best for all without having to kill the other team. Coexistence is the answer to cooperative effort.

The Money Game

In my book "Instructions To Money" I applied the basic ideas of successful small business to address the problem of how to gain wealth and play by the rules of the game.

In that book I shared some of the secrets of wealth building that have been withheld to the general population for years and showed how I could go from poverty to a upper middle class life style and do it honestly. I showed how anyone could be given the tools to become a millionaire if they were just willing to do what it takes to set goals and work a plan to achieve the goals of passive income and owning the means of production.

Thousands of the book sold and many wrote me of their successes and some of their trials in finding the right way to overcome poverty. Along the way I found another author who wrote a similar book entitled "Welfare to Millionaire" and she was a democrat. We shared for years links, efforts, and web promotion and radio and TV PR contacts in helping each other to be successful.

During my research for my book, and recounting my story, I called the US Government Treasury and asked them one question which is revealing about the nature of this game called money that we have all agreed to play together.

That question was how much real cost is there to print one one hundred dollar bill? According to the US Government Mint it costs us only 6¢ (six cents) to print one one hundred dollar bill. That means that if you have in real value $60,000 in one hundred dollar bills in your pocket that you have one million dollars in face value. So in the money game we all pretend that $60,000 of printed paper is one million dollars. In history when mankind had no money, they would barter or exchange goods to complete transactions and meet there needs.

But in order to form a more common exchange method, world governments formed this system where we exchange paper and coins in place of goods so that we can all have a method of exchange that all can work with and agree on.

This might seem obvious to even talk about but it is important to know that we are all playing games here and in fact have created our own reality in doing these things in governments and in banking systems. If we had all grown into a society with different means of exchange it might seem strange to us to have such a system as money or that everyone would agree with this system without having first gotten together and planned it out.

Yet by chance and just progress, we have the system of money that we have today.

So when I looked at the rules of how we govern our monetary system, I found that we have a loophole that is open wide that allows for anyone to gain wealth and do it by the rules.

The Idea I came up with is called the REESA and I shall line it out in this book so you can understand what it is and why it is the only solution to answer all the worlds money problems.

Energy and Resources

It is the personal problems of life that are the true mother of invention and from one idea we can gain other ideas that can dream up new technology and science that can make a better world for all. Building the better mouse trap is not just because we want to gain wealth selling it, but because we have a mouse problem.

As I wrote earlier in this book my son is disabled. As a result of his muscles progressively getting weaker, he has had to go on a vent breathing system and several pieces of electric equipment which have been added to my home to help him stay alive.
Along with this equipment comes a bigger electric bill and most months due to his needs I am paying about $550 in Electric costs.

So with energy you can see that I had a need to find a better mouse trap to solve the problem of my money going in large amounts to the electric bill each month.

In government they say that if I am low income that they will subsidize my bill and give me about $300 every year to help pay my electric bill. With over $6000 in costs for electric each year that resource of government money would not even come close to meeting my needs. My son's social security check is even lower than that amount monthly and can not even pay for the electric bills I get monthly. So government social welfare programs have no solution and even if the left wing democrats wanted to pay all my electric bill there would not be enough money to solve this problem even if everyone was taxed at 100%

We have seen the proof of this concept in the 16 Trillion dollar debt that the US Government has racked up over the last few years. The idea of a debt based economic system looks good on paper but in actual application it has become a nightmare.

We can continue to point fingers and play who done it games but that will not solve the problem. As the old saying goes, "your part of the problem or part of the solution."

So in the climate of need, I came up with a solution to my energy problem that works and will not only pay my electric bills, but also pay me back money for implementing the solution.

The use of HHO generators can give me Hydrogen to burn in a propane based electric generator. That will create more electric than I need, and thereby solve the problem of an expense and turn it into an income. As with government, business, and personal life the problem is resources and this book is the answer to that problem.

2 REESA Solution

In the course of human events when a people find that the ties that bind them must be broken and the economic slavery of the people must be ended, it is important to not just adopt the words of the Declaration of Independence to address this course, but to also truly find a way to overcome those political and economic ties necessary to be broken and form a new structure whereby freedom may be obtained.

Our economic independence will have to change everything about our rules and structure and still keep in place the game by which we all agreed to play. In doing so we will find critics that will say that this or that is why it can not be done, but never give good reasons for not doing it.

The no-communists and the neoconservatives will all find fault with this idea, yet they can not deny that rich men have used it over and over to solve problems that otherwise had no solution.

Many real estate millionaires have used this as did the country of Sierra Leone to solve monetary problems and with my method it can be done with zero cost to the tax payer and zero cost to the government in actual income taxes.

PRA - Personal REESA Accounts

The REESA is a Retirement Emergency Education Savings Account thus the acronym REESA.

Do not let the idea savings account chase you away because **it is not a traditional answer that the conservatives have offered before.** A REESA is an account that is like an IRA but without the restrictions of earnings or benefits that tradition IRA accounts have and with additional restrictions and rules that will prevent the economy from going into sky rocketing inflation.
Keep an open mind and allow me to explain how it works.
The REESA is designed to supply the needs of society in a capitalist based economy providing the following frame work of advantages over the present system:

1. It pays for it self and requires no up front cost or tax so no government expenses are incurred other than to pass legislation.

2. It places funds into the private sector from which the economy can grow.

3. It uses financial institutions in place so no new infrastructure is required to implement the program.

4. It uses methods that investors have used for

years to solve funding and finance problems.

5. It only requires regulations to insure that inflation is not a factor in the economic system to prevent unwanted outcomes.

The bases is the use of U S Treasury Zero Coupon Bonds to fund a self liquidating loan similar to the methods use by many financial experts in the private sector and in world banking.

The need for funding of retirement and social services for any person is going to be paid for in either taxes or in investments. There is no other way to deal with the problems of modern society.

So many have used these types of loans to fund real estate projects, public works in foreign countries, and operating expenses in business in the past.

Step one to a REESA is to determine the cost of the Bonds to fund two million dollars in return at the end of 30 to 40 years.

A US Treasury Zero Coupon bond is like a savings bond which gains value in interest in the same way. The average cost of the bonds for a return of $1000 in 30 years is about $250 plus brokerage costs and that value may vary with the market.

So to obtain our 2 million in bonds at face value in

30 years we would need about $500,000

At 5% for 30 years the payment would equal $2684.11 a month or $32209.32 a year. The life of the loan the bank would get $966,279.60 for the loan in principal and interest.

Now we have our Base operating expense we can now give the bonds at the value of 2 million dollars to the bank which is dispersed as a simultaneous closing where the bonds are issued and $1,000,000 is place in a savings account at 5% interest for 30 years with the interest compounding for the life of the account.

The other one million in bond face value will go to pay for the loan of $500,000 to obtain the bonds.

In 30 years the bank or financial institution will invest the money created in this account into funding small business, housing, industry, and local economic needs on secured financing and return to the account annually 5% so as to compound the total savings interest which will result in a stimulus to the economy and growth through grass roots economic support for job creation.

In 30 years the interest and principal will grow to a total of $4,321,942.38

Now to insure that the tax payers do not foot the

bill, we account for the costs of this plan on the 30th birthday of the account as follows:

$966,279.60 of the account goes to the bank for the half a million loan for the bonds.

$33,720.40 goes to the US Treasury as a funding fee.
$1 Million goes to the bank in surrender for the principal amount of the savings account. Balance of the savings account is now at $2,321,942.38 for retirement of which only the annual interest in part can be used for retirement purposes at the normal income tax rate.

Total tax cost $0 ! Total earnings the the US Government for the 350 million accounts for everyone is $11,802,140,000,000
That is 11 Trillion Dollars to fund a balanced budget. The US Government can use these funds to reduce the money supply every 30 years and adjust the economic factors for interest and inflation.

No more legislators going to raid the trust fund, just simple math that solves problems and funds efforts to get things done.

To insure that inflation does not devalue the dollar, we put a annual cap on what can come out of the account for retirement and allow the interest in the account to fund Social Security benefits for the account owner in case of emergency or disability.

For the life of the account, we set those benefits at $320,000 which is equal to about $11,000 a year to fund health insurance costs or disability payments if required in the individual case.

After 15 years of the account we allow $5,000 for each year to be taken out in one lump sum for education for children in the amount of $75,000.00

Social Security Continues but is funded in a tax at the income level from paychecks for working but payments in benefits are shifted over time to the REESA account for funding of payments.

Thus we have supplied for the funding of all social services such as food stamps, welfare, and assistance for handicap from the incoming taxes for social security and then reduce that cost each year as the progression of REESA accounts provide for the needs of these special benefits.

The principal amounts of $2 million at 30 years may not ever be withdrawn to insure that the account is funded, and to keep control of the economy for inflation. The Federal reserve will set a cost of living funding amount to give the annual amount of retirement funding such as the interest rate will allow and taxes will permit to give a retired person enough to enjoy their life and allow for any additional needs to be covered.

Let's say the two million yields interest at $50 thousand per million and there has been no adjustment in the rate for the account by legislation which will give us $100,000 to use for retirement and reinvestment at age 65.

The UST REESA rate might be set at $60,000 for the year with a 10% income tax of $10,000 on the interest which will leave $40 thousand to accrue in interest for the account.

Upon the death of the person, their REESA will then be distributed to the children of the account owner and added to their REESA which brings us to the economic growth phase of the plan under REESA.

BRA - Business REESA Accounts

A Business REESA allows business to grow and can be funded by a financial institution by one of two methods:

1. Death Beneficiary overage or

2. New established REESA funding.

A person who has a good idea, or wants to open say a bakery, or plant making goods for sale to the public comes to the bank with a great business plan. The bank sets up a REESA to fund the project and allows the interest to be paid out on a monthly bases of 50% of the interest to insure the success of the business. Risk and reward factors can then be tested by the market demand and the results of poor funded project with US Government loans will be removed in that the BRA has absorbed the risks that SBA funding once took on. No more failed solar power companies that the Tax payer pays for.

RRA - Real Estate REESA

Multi-unit funding can now be shifted with community development or private investment programs to a RRA to insure that the real estate market remains stable and commensurate with the cost of building. the biggest error of the CRA (Community Reinvestment Act) was that it forced banks to fund loans for real estate that the borrower could not pay back. Financial institutions got overpriced values based on the trend of real estate values going up over the past and then when the funding was sold in package investment to the wall street market the whole thing crashed due to over regulation that lead to unreal appraisals.

To build a 1000 square foot home it cost in real building material and labor about one dollar a square foot. The land cost added to that given the area of the home, and you had a real cost to replace or build that home. The appraisals should always use as the based the real value of this cost and then give an added value based on area or no value based on where the building is going.

If real legislation was put in place for RRA the economy of scale could set actual values and bring back the building industry by funding it with REESA accounts and by regulating the appraisers to put a real base value on the building without inflating the values to get funding. The CRA can then be administered to the rich and poor evenly so as to allow a chance for everyone to own a home and gain profits in investment equally.

GRA - Government REESA

The Governments of states or federal agencies could fund their projects approved by congress with a REESA account also that would open the door to make benefits to the world by opening markets and resources to all people through government REESA programs.

We could fund water wells in Africa, or playgrounds in Cleveland with a REESA and then allow for the account to fund the maintaining of the project. I can think of thousands of things such as funding roads, NASA, and even the US Armed Forces with a special GRA.

ETA - Emerging Technology REESA

The problem with energy is that we have become depended on burning it. Burning energy is not a wise use of the exchange of the physics of energy and ends in a bad outcome in the final chapter of the story of mankind and energy.

No matter what side of the political spectrum you live on, we all know that once all the oil is used, all the uranium is spent, and the water is all gone, we have no place to go but the way of the dinosaurs.

I would like to think that we all could agree that we want the earth to survive with our great grandchildren into eternity future with a good method of production of heat and food so that the environment will be clean and we can pass on to future generations that blessings we have enjoyed.

One of the best ways to fund HHO production methods is to use a ERA to fund the building of the grid for electric generation at the grass roots level and give all Americans a share in the production of the growing need for energy for industry and business.

HHO is the method of splitting water and burning the Hydrogen and Oxygen in small amount to power generators and electric generations systems. It has also been used to replace Gasoline in combustion engines and burns cleaner and using less fuel. A visit to YouTube with the search HHO will show lots of what is being done today by garage inventors who have found the power of energy that is all around us.

Searl Magnetic's of California has also developed a unit that can use static electric physics to create vast amounts of electric energy to power homes and businesses using a device called the SEG.

The SEG uses rare earth magnets to gather through coils electric without burning fossil fuels.

The device can also fly and create it's own gravity so as to suggest that light speed travel is achievable.

The use of the SEG in air and space travel, as well as generating power, can be proven to revolutionize the world and make the possible migration of man into space a reality by funding these new emerging technologies with ERA accounts.

Many of these new Energy Ideas are based on the works of Stan Meyer and others who have pioneered in magnetism and physics that has proven a beneficial asset to even the development of top secret designs for air and space use. The Hydrogen production unit for the Mars mission was based on the work of Stan Meyer who had patents in Laser water splitting and other HHO systems.

REESA Legislation

The use of proper regulations and laws can prevent

an over inflation of the economy by using the best methods of capitalism to fund the best ideals of our charity and compassion to others, and do so without destroying the cooperation of those with different points of view.

I believe that an ear of peace can come to America from using these innovative ideas to overcome disagreements and to allow all to peruse life, liberty, and happiness in self fulfilling labor and do so while feeding the creative mind in us all to become united again. In all honesty we all know that we can not find common ground unless we remove the funding of things which goes against our nature through forced taxation by allowing the resources to come from somewhere other than the pocket of the tax payer. When we all fund our own brand of healthcare from our own REESA accounts, then the right will be at peace that they will not have to do what is spiritually against their morals, and the left will be happy that they can get what they want to without having to fight the right to get what they think should be.

No more battles for any class, and all have a true safety net to allow the best part of the economic system to provide for the nation and it's people without breaking the bank to do it.

CRA - Charity RESSA

As a final note, you may also consider the funding

of Charity via a REESA account for Non-profit groups and organizations that will provide for a long term support of the things which have made us great as Americans, our faith and our charitable nature to even feed and help our enemies in time of trouble or disaster.

We as a nation have done more in disaster assistance than any nation in history, and are more charitable than all other societies.
Funding charity with REESA accounts is not just a good idea, it is the best foreign policy and community action that we can do to build a better future at home and abroad.

There is no doubt that this idea will meet some resistance, but once it is understood and implemented, the future of mankind and this nation will become only limited by what we can imagine and the possibilities are endless in what this one idea may begin. If we just use this to give every child a college education, what a dream. The only thing I know for sure is that this is true, a quote from my book of 1996 Instructions To Money:

"They only way to surly fail, is never really try"

If you do not try, you can never learn what works and never overcome any challenge. The greatest mind with the greatest ideas that were never tried, were bound to fail, and failure was in not doing.

With that in mind, I hope to get this book to every legislature in the federal and state government that I have the resources to provide. It is not a political thing, it is a wisdom thing and a trying thing. I believe this is the only valid solution to solve taxation and debt problems for this country. Teaching others to use capitalism to socialize profits to benefit all is not new, foundations and organizations do it every day of the week. Just applying it to such a scale for the benefit of mankind, that is something worth trying. But in truth, this is just what a broker of stocks does every day, teach people to buy a share in the dividends of corporate profits to fund 401K account and retirement. Now if we can use it to fund ideas and greatness we will have progressed to the next level of man's growth toward the future and the stars. The beauty of this whole concept is that we do not have to get everyone to agree with our point of view to do this, we just have to get everyone to agree with what works.

Alternative Energy that works-See on the internet:
http://searlmagnetics.com/
http://info-etudiants.com/videos/?v=StV4jkJPnDY
http://geetinternational.com/Patent%2096014501_000001.pdf
http://www.youtube.com/watch?v=2xHvEsUv0wg
http://www.youtube.com/watch?v=ka0E12gQ9eQ&feature=related
http://www.youtube.com/watch?v=OXctY1K4wko&feature=related

SUMMARY OF POLICY Economic Justice.

The problems of compromise in a deadlocked political situation always results in some sort of coup of power. In the former Soviet Union we have seen these factions gain and lose power when one or another covert group work secretly to remove their opposing political group. Over the recent history we have seen Russian operatives use Agent Orange, dioxin, to attempt to kill the Ukrainian President, and even use radioactive material to target people for murder. These attempts to influence power in politics is not without notice, and likely will never be solved as to "who done it". We should never underestimate our enemies as we find solutions from within. The Cold War may be over but many battles for the hearts and minds is still on going.

Some policies are unpopular, but in time become generally accepted as the right thing to do. In the Civil War the policies of Lincoln were not popular in the south, but in looking back, even though Lincoln was a Republican, the shift of claim to the party that favors the freedoms of African Americans has become the Democrats who were in fact formed by the white slave owners of the south.

The message of the party has become that of influence as it has been defined by the opposition in this case. The greatest problem is not that African Americans do not have enough freedom, or that minorities do not have opportunity in the United States, but that what has become known as reverse racism has been allowed to prevail in many unspoken segments of society. The Black Panthers, and other groups of militant anti-white groups such as those who foster deep violent hate and neo-muslim black supremacists have as of yet gone unanswered by more reasonable voices in society and government.

Anti Mexican and Anti Black separatists such as Randy Weaver has been met by government actions that overstepped the boundaries of law by killing his family which resulted in a law suit which Randy Weaver won against the US Government.

These racial issues have never truly been addressed to the point of bringing harmony and reconciliation to both whites, blacks, and the many shades of color in between. This is the root of the idea of social justice which is in fact impossible to solve without three key elements.

1. All must agree to abandon their hate and truly mean it.
2. All must be educated in the facts of DNA and biology that proves we are all from the same tree of man that began with one man and one woman.
3. All must learn that violent solutions to disagreements kills the work of love.

In my own family I have Mexican Americans, Irish Americans, Ukrainian Americans, African Americans, and so on. My own DNA proves that I am a Jewish, Welsh, Irish, African, Hebrew, Ukrainian, German with a mix of about half of the known countries of the world. As a conservative, the left would expect me to be some sort of self-hater who is not kind or loving to those that are even in my own blood. That is because of dehumanization of the message by the opposition to the real message I bring.

Some policies that the Conservatives can bring to the table that would change this view would be controversial, but helpful to the total resolution to the problem of hate, and make this nation in its progression to a better union overcome the deep anger and bitterness of hate based on color of skin.

The left also needs to stop demonizing the right as a racist organization and admit that Martin Luther King and Lincoln were both Republicans.

Since this plan, the RESSA, will solve much of the social injustice that has been the forefront of the battle lines between the left and right, then other issues can be addressed with this summary in mind. Economic Justice is a perspective point of view. It is not how it has been defined, but how it is achieved and understood.

One such issue is the boarder of the US and

Mexico. We all want free trade with free nations and should have resolved this issue long ago. I would suggest that we make Mexico an offer of Statehood and give them a chance to become the 52nd State.

In the last election Porto Rico voted to become a state in the United States. This would balance the stars on the flag and allow for a much smaller boarder to defend at the tip of Mexico and would allow for the population which is here in the United States to become unified into what is already become part of American society.

Some conservatives would resist this, but as a conservative myself, I think much of this could be overcome by compromises in other agreements in the process. The RESSA solves the financial issue and that would seem to trump the other issues. Many would have a RESSA to start businesses and create revenue that will raise the tax income by volume which is a basic tenant of Reagan's economic plan which Clinton used to great effect to balance the budget.

Finally I offer this summary, If means is no longer an issue, then why would we need to fight? Healing of the soul could happen if we just stopped the hate and argument long enough to hug.

So I propose a Hug not Hate day. On this day we would hug instead of hate each other over our differences and thereby resolve the anger inside with love inside. Let's all put to a final rest the racial issues in the United States and mutually become a family as a nation rather than allow hate to rip us apart. Otherwise we will have forgotten the first law of war and fail to stop it from destroying us as a people. That is the law which says divide and conquer. If we remain divided, we shall be to weak to resist being conquered by our enemies or consumed by our own hate.

John 13:34 A new commandment I give unto you, That ye love one another; as I have loved you, that ye also love one another.

There is no monopoly on good ideas. We have seen this in many such debates on issues that have yielded solutions to problems that have shown the possibilities in different approaches. One such solution was brought up by Governor Romney in this last election during the debates. The idea of a doctrinal infiltration into the Muslim religion to argue the perspective of jihad as one where we remove sin from our own lives and allow repentance in others rather than force Islamic conversions. In history we see from the Spanish Inquisitions that the Catholic Church eventually repented from forced conversions at the threat of the sword when the ideas of the message of love found in the scriptures trumped the call for war against sinners.

In Jewish history we see similar calls to remove the nations of idol worship and spare none, yet Judaism has become a more tolerant nation of it's own Islamic and Christian citizens.

The bases of all resolve in these matters should be that in the end God will judge and not man. Without life there is no hope of repentance from sin and no resolution of injustice. If we can all agree that to do the right thing for the lives of our children and the prosperity of our mutual nations and races of people can be done, then I for one am content to let God be God and not judge unto death another who does not hold my religious views.

We must not assume that if we find tolerance in our point of views that we will not stand against evil, but rather that it is not our job to put an end to evil, just provide a way of escape from evil so that we can let God be the judge over it. When we take a life into our own hands such as the terrorists did on 9-11 we do all mankind a disservice in passing judgment without due process of a trial before God himself. As a Great Messiah said in the Bible, let him without sin cast the first stone. If that was our practice as humans, no one would be stoned, for we all have sinned.

To ignore that militant Islam is a religious threat to peace first, is to not see reality and allow appeasement and surrender by attrition. The issue is Religious doctrine and best answered there.

Conclusion

In closing, I would like to say that the racial issues in the inner city black community must be addressed by all society. Black on Black crime and murder is at higher rates than white on white crime in the numbers of crimes and acts of violence. In comparison, black on white crimes is higher and the ideals of reverse radical neomuslim inspired racial separatism taught in black churches and religious groups is nothing less than a new form of apatite doctrine.

The Black community in America must reject this confrontational point of view and learn to forgive and forget the past vengeance and wrongs done by whites. Get over it. Whites also need to put behind the acts of violence of blacks and be willing to communicate in community meetings and help remove the influences together that threaten to destroy communities. If we all would work together to stop gang violence and clean up the inner cities where these events happen, then we can overcome the drugs and violence that is causing disunity.

The REESA allows us to gain community based action committees that can address needs for drug rehab, assistance to help those in need to form joint businesses and community groups that can put an end to poverty and put an end to those who prey on the weak and uneducated to exploit them for selfish gain.

Sin must be addressed as sin, and solutions found to bring love, education, knowledge, and wisdom into a unified America that can be as strong as possible and righteous in deeds and actions for all the people in equal distribution of opportunity.

REESA can restore the control of the people to hold our basic morals again in high regard and pass on to the next generation the hope and love that self respect and pride in achievement gives to those who find the pursuit of happiness to be a mutual goal of all people.

My hope and prayer is that all who read this will help get it into the hands of their leaders and use this idea to begin a new era of cooperation and success in life for us all.

President Ronald Reagan said "Communism is the mutual inherited sharing of poverty". History has shown that creativity and prosperity is destroyed in equalization of reward for both non productive and productive individuals.

When rewards are equal for the efforts of differing degrees, it is human nature to see work as pointless. The same is true when taxation is overbearing and regulation inhibits growth and efforts. People just give up and only do the least possible work to survive and avoid being noticed by the increasing laws that limit them from achievement and takes from them the pride and riches that they deserve as a just paycheck for their labors. Unions, Governments, and nanny state regulations at all levels destroy the creativity of mankind and their desire to dream, work, and set goals.

If this is true, a fact of human nature, then the opposite is true also that Capitalism is the mutual inherited sharing of wealth with each progression of mankind's generations. The REESA can reward prosperity by funding ideas that can solve the problems and needs of the future, and do it creating a capital base of economic opportunity the rewards those who are willing to risk financial security and replace it with mutual prosperity, education, creativity, and stability of efforts of cooperative teams who can achieve scientific advances and communities with industry who own the means of production and escape the slavery of poverty.

When a regulation or a law is just, it protects the rights of the people and gives them desire and inspiration to achieve great things. When the opposite is true, it destroys growth. If we allow our resource to be dissolved into the pages of history as a byword of societies that failed, we are in grave danger of dissolving even the record of our being here. We must change our attitude or that is our fate.

National Lottery.

The final solution I want to propose, and share with you is that of a national lottery. Gambling small amount for a big payoff is allowed in many states and has become a source of income for governments to care for handicap people, elderly, and for other benefits which citizens can support as a form of charity. Many states allow bingo, raffle tickets, and bake sales which are a gamble in not knowing what is in much of the sugar filled treats that we buy to support our faith, causes, and even funds to help the sick.

A national lottery, sold internationally, could generate as much as one billion in sales world wide. Since some would complain about it cutting into state run lottery revenues, it could be limited to a once a month program with a price of maybe as much as $10 a ticket. With 340 million Americans, that would be over 3 billion in sales. If taken to the internet, and international sales, the potential of 1 billion sales would mean over 10 trillion dollars in a year. IF the congress and the senate did not mess up the idea with phoney pork spending, and put the money on the national debt first, a prize of 50 million or more would become a norm for a monthly pot. Lower prizes also could be awarded and this could be earmarked for national debt and healthcare subsidized premiums alone, allowing for the cost of national health care to be returned to the people, and target for help only those who could not afford healthcare due to preconditions and poverty. This would make the tax mandates and the penalties in Obamacare to go away with the death panels and the other cost effective items. By putting these plans into operation and revoking the present system which everyone hates, even the leftists, the new national health care and lottery act could solve the problems that make so many angry about what the law as it is now has caused in failed businesses, poor economic conditions, and the prescription to crash the world economy and the dollar. If nothing is done, then this is the only results that the unaffordable health care act could cause.

Millions are now on the internet as you read this signing pledges to not comply with the new law. Even democrats are calling it socialism and communism. They are angry that they will have to pay big premiums and high deductibles. They are angry that their doctors are running away from this act and what it will mean to their business. Obama has proposed a plan of sharing the wealth and spreading it around which adds up to nothing more than what soviet style socialism was, the inherited mutual sharing of poverty. We all go broke and get poor. The jobs go away and the growth goes to nothing.

No one wants to start a new business or invest in ideas because the rewards of doing such will be costs and taxes above the possible earnings and profits. Shareholders will not invest in companies that are doomed to lose their money, and even Unions will not have a retirement plan to overcome the greatest expenses in the negative bottom line. The Democrats have failed bitterly in their new liberal model of America. They have isolated the majority of Americans, and lost touch with reality.

The only way to change things is to flip the coin so to speak, and teach our youth the benefits of the mutual inherited sharing of wealth through hard work, and owning the means of production as a marketer of goods through small businesses as an entrepreneur. The only way to cut taxes with the incompetent stupid lawyers and commies in Washington DC is to fire them and put plans into place that will restore trust worthy service in the officials we vote for. To do that, they will have to stop doing what they always have to fail and wonder why the insane ideas of dong the same things is not working. Change the plan, change the mind, change the results.

With a REESA and a National Lottery you end the debate on national healthcare, taxation, and move on to issues that will help mankind better himself. When a person wants to own a business, and has a plan that can work, and the proper skills and education to reach for their goals and achieve greatness, the American has never let the world down, and will always find a way in the greatest odds to overcome failure. To do so you must first acknowledge you were wrong, and recover from the defeat. Our economy and the world economy is suffering from the defeat of the socialistic ideals and the communist practices of governments.

The Marxist idea was great in theory, but has failed in practice. It always will because to really share everything and still produce enough, you must have some motivation other than the big nanny state says so and points a gun at you to force you to buy their controlling system and care for you, when you know, they are no different than anyone who is looking out for themselves first.

It is not the greed of businessmen and women that makes the system fail, it is the greed of governments that want to control the free market and be the overbearing nanny that has to do everything for us.

My proposals are just the only untried solutions that are yet tested by the capitalist model. Those who have distributed the wealth in great amount in a mixture of capitalist and communist theories, have all crashed their economic models and gone down in flames.

Prices and inflation destroy the benefits of the wealth distribution. then we see what happened in South America when rice was priced at thousand of dollars a bag.

Only with economic controls that are reasonable, and with plans to stimulate individual capitalistic ventures, can the turn around happen for America and the world. It is not the cooperation or the corporation that has caused this to fail, but the ignorance of the socialists in ivory towers who thought that the Russians just did it wrong, or that some how we can force social justice to solve all injustices. The only way to change a person is from within the heart. The American always is charitable when given the resources to create wealth and thus feel blessed, and desire to help others. That is the nature of Americans.

That is why communist models that the democrats want to force on us will always fail. It is in our nature to just sit down and do nothing rather than be forced to pay for someone who is not willing to help himself. Poor as he or she may be, the reward must be equal to or greater in the work and business venture, or like the first Mayflower settlers, they will under produce when forced to share.

Only when our forefather Gov Bradford gave each family and person some land to own for themselves, did the bounty of hard work reward the exchange of goods in a barter and trade system that has been the bedrock of what worked and always will work in America, because it has for over 400 years.

Even Kings and Potentates who have discovered this about human nature, have had successful reigns and rule, and found not just reward in greater income for the crown, but also in the love of the people for finding what works and allowing them to become kings in their own castles.

The entrepreneur model of owners of production, and the creators of wealth, is what made the past successes work, and with plans like the ones I proposed here, the inspiration of greatness can be once more the American dream.

Stimulate the growth at the grass roots, and watch what happens when the people have liberty to make their own destiny.

If you want solutions, do not feed them fish, but teach them to fish, and how to start a fish farm, and grow more fish, and then the world will be feed fish and the profit will be bountiful and the excess will be blessings to the next generation.

Generational wealth for all is possible and can make the dreams of our childhood the true life adventure of our adulthood.

May all your dreams of success and greatness come true, and my you find the peace and happiness that our constitution says is your God given right to pursue.

MERRICK REESA ENERGY SOLUTION

The Solution To Government and Business Resources

BY:

Daniel W. Merrick, Ph.D.

© 2012 Daniel W. Merrick, PhD;

**Eternal Light & Power Company Publishing
PO BOX 1533 Smethport, Pennsylvania 16749-1533**

EternalLightAndPowerCompany.Org

ISBN-13: 978-1494843663

ISBN-10: 1494843668

www.ingramcontent.com/pod-product-compliance
Lightning Source LLC
Chambersburg PA
CBHW071817170526
45167CB00003B/1344